WHALES

Rebecca Woodbury, Ph.D., M.Ed.

Gravitas Publications Inc.

WHALES

Illustrations: Janet Moneymaker

Copyright © 2025 by Rebecca Woodbury, Ph.D., M.Ed.

All rights reserved. No part of this publication may be reproduced, stored in a retrieval system, or transmitted, in any form or by any means, electronic, mechanical, photocopying, recording, or otherwise, without prior written permission from the publisher. No part of this book may be reproduced in any manner whatsoever without written permission.

Whales
ISBN 978-1-950415-70-0

Published by Gravitas Publications Inc.
Imprint: Real Science-4-Kids
www.gravitaspublications.com
www.realscience4kids.com

 Photo credits: Cover & Title Pg: By Craig Lambert Photo, AdobeStock; Above–NOAA, Public Domain; P.3. NOAA NMFS AKFSC; P.7. Jeremy Bezanger on Unsplash; P.9: Top, Fabrizio Frigeni on Unsplash; Bottom, Dr. Mridula Srinivasan, NOAA/NMFS/OST/AMD; P11. Jacqueline Schmid from Pixabay; P.13. NASA, Public Domain; P.15. Dr. Louis M. Herman, NOAA; P.17. Top, Randall Wade (Rand) Grant from Vancouver, Canada, CC BY SA 2.0; Bottom, Personnel of NOAA Ship RAINIER; P.19: Top, NOAA, Public Domain; Bottom, Øystein Paulsen, CC BY SA 3.0; P.21. Brandon Sok on Unsplash

Whales are animals that live only in water. Most types of whales live in the ocean but a few live in rivers.

That looks like fun.

Orcas

Whales are **mammals**. They are in a group of mammals called **cetaceans**.

What are: MAMMALS?

Mammals are animals that breathe air, feed milk to their babies, and have fur for at least part of their life. Most mammals give birth to live babies.

What are: CETACEANS?

Cetaceans are mammals that spend all their time in water. Air is taken in through one or two **blowholes** on top of the head. Cetaceans must come to the surface of the water often so they can take in air through their blowholes.

Whales usually travel in groups called **pods.** They talk to each other with clicks, whistles, squeaks, and squawks.

Dolphins

There are two types of whales:

- Whales with teeth.

- Whales without teeth.

Dolphins have teeth

Humpback whales do not have teeth

Whales that have teeth eat
fish, squid, crabs, and shrimp.

I use teeth to eat cheese!

Orca

Whales use blowholes to breathe air in and out. A blowhole is on top of a whale's head.

Whales with teeth have one blowhole on top of the head.

I wonder what it is like to breathe through the top of your head?

Dolphin

Whales without teeth have two blowholes on top of the head.

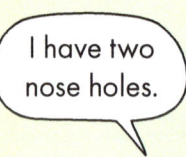

Humpback whale blowholes

Whales without teeth have **baleen** bristles instead of teeth. A baleen plate is a comb-like structure that hangs down from the top jaw.

A baleen whale takes in a mouthful of water. Then it pushes the water out through the baleen. Food is caught in the baleen and licked off by the whale.

Baleen

Baleen

Humpback whale

The biggest animal on Earth is the blue whale, which is a baleen whale. It mainly eats tiny animals called krill.

Blue whale

Krill

There is much more to learn about whales and other underwater animals.

What do you think it is like to live in a part of the world that is so much different than where we live?

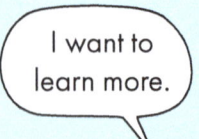# I want to learn more.

Dolphins

How to say science words

baleen   (buh-LEEN)

blowhole   (BLOH-hohl)

bristle   (BRIH-suhl)

cetacean   (sih-TAY-shuhn)

dolphin   (DAHL-fuhn)

mammal   (MAA-muhl)

pod   (PAHD)

science   (SIY-uhns)

whale   (WAYL)

www.ingramcontent.com/pod-product-compliance
Lightning Source LLC
Chambersburg PA
CBHW041632040426
42446CB00022B/3490